Should Students Go to

SCHOOL

All Year Round?

By Elizabeth Morgan

KidHaven PUBLISHING

Published in 2019 by
KidHaven Publishing, an Imprint of Greenhaven Publishing, LLC
353 3rd Avenue
Suite 255
New York, NY 10010

Designer: Deanna Paternostro
Editor: Katie Kawa

Photo credits: Cover Syda Productions/Shutterstock.com; pp. 5, 21 (inset, middle-left) Sergey Novikov/Shutterstock.com; p. 7 Monkey Business Images/Shutterstock.com; p. 9 wavebreakmedia/ Shutterstock.com; p. 11 iofoto/Shutterstock.com; p. 13 stockfour/Shutterstock.com; p. 15 (top) tammykayphoto/Shutterstock.com; p. 15 (bottom) Africa Studio/Shutterstock.com; p. 17 (top) hxdbzxy/Shutterstock.com; p. 17 (bottom) spass/Shutterstock.com; p. 19 Robert Elias/ Shutterstock.com; p. 21 (notepad) ESB Professional/Shutterstock.com; p. 21 (markers) Kucher Serhii/ Shutterstock.com; p. 21 (photo frame) FARBAI/iStock/Thinkstock; p. 21 (inset, left) Tom Wang/ Shutterstock.com; p. 21 (inset, middle-right) Pressmaster/Shutterstock.com; p. 21 (inset, right) Robert Kneschke/Shutterstock.com.

Cataloging-in-Publication Data

Names: Morgan, Elizabeth.
Title: Should students go to school all year round? / Elizabeth Morgan.
Description: New York : KidHaven Publishing, 2019. | Series: Points of view | Includes glossary and index.
Identifiers: ISBN 9781534525566 (pbk.) | 9781534525559 (library bound) | ISBN 9781534525573 (6 pack) | ISBN 9781534525580 (ebook)
Subjects: LCSH: Year-round schools–United States. | School management and organization–United States.
Classification: LCC LB3034.M854 2019 | DDC 371.2'36–dc23

Printed in the United States of America

CPSIA compliance information: Batch #BS18KL: For further information contact Greenhaven Publishing LLC, New York, New York at 1-844-317-7404.

Please visit our website, www.greenhavenpublishing.com. For a free color catalog of all our high-quality books, call toll free 1-844-317-7404 or fax 1-844-317-7405.

CONTENTS

No Summer Vacation?   **4**

A Different Way of Doing Things   **6**

Less Time to Forget   **8**

Does It Really Help?   **10**

Good for Students and Teachers   **12**

Staying Busy in the Summer   **14**

Helping with Overcrowding   **16**

Extra Costs   **18**

Looking at Both Sides   **20**

Glossary   **22**

For More Information   **23**

Index   **24**

No Summer
VACATION?

Most students in the United States don't have to go to school during the summer months. However, did you know that some students don't have long summer vacations? They go to school all year round—with a few short breaks instead of one long break.

Some people believe that going to school all year is good for students and teachers. Other people believe summer vacations are important. People on both sides of this **debate** use different facts to back up their arguments. Read on to learn more about these different points of view!

Know the Facts!

The length of a school year in the United States is generally between 170 and 180 days.

Is it better for students to have a summer vacation or to go to school all year? Learning the facts before answering a question is an important part of having an informed, or educated, opinion.

A Different Way of
DOING THINGS

The most recent major study of year-round education in the United States took place in 2012. At that time, 3,700 public schools across the country were year-round schools.

Year-round schools don't have much longer school years than **traditional** schools. They just break up the year differently. Instead of one big break in the summer, they have smaller breaks throughout the year. A common year-round schooling calendar features 45 days of teaching followed by 15 days off. Others include 60 days of teaching followed by 20 days off and 90 days of teaching followed by 30 days off.

Know the Facts!

Some year-round schools work on a single track, in which all students have the same breaks. Others use a multi-track method, in which groups of teachers and students have breaks at different times.

Students who go to year-round schools still have weekends off and still go to school for around 180 days each year.

Less Time to
FORGET

Some people believe every student should go to school all year round. One of the main reasons they believe this is because they feel summer vacations are too long. For students who don't go to school all year round, summer vacations generally last from June to September.

People who want to shorten summer vacations worry about students forgetting what they learned because they're away from school for so long. They believe shorter breaks give students less time to forget. This means teachers won't have to spend as much time in class **reviewing** facts from the year before.

Know the Facts!

According to the newspaper *Education Week*, two-thirds of American teachers spend at least one month reviewing when students come back from summer vacation.

Some people believe going to school all year round allows teachers to spend more time on new lessons and less time reviewing forgotten facts.

Does It Really
HELP?

With less time to forget things, it seems to make sense that year-round schooling would lead to better grades for students. However, studies have shown mixed results about the connection between shorter summer breaks and higher grades.

People often want to know for sure that year-round schooling is good for students before making such a big change. Some teachers have argued that year-round schooling could actually lead to more time spent reviewing. This is because year-round schools often have three breaks that last three weeks, and students need to review after those breaks, too.

Know the Facts!

In 2002, 227 public schools in Los Angeles, California, were open all year round. By 2015, only one of those schools was still a year-round school.

Different studies of year-round schooling have produced different results. This makes it hard to know if year-round schooling helps students.

Good for Students and
TEACHERS

Although some people argue that more breaks could be bad for learning, others believe adding in short breaks throughout the year is helpful. Students and teachers sometimes deal with burnout when they only have one long vacation. This means that they're working too hard and aren't able to do their best because they need a break. Year-round schooling allows for more breaks, which can ease burnout.

Many people also believe that children get bored when their summer vacations are too long. Year-round schooling helps keep that from happening.

Know the Facts!

According to a 2017 study, 61 percent of teachers and other school staff said their job is **stressful**.

Some people believe year-round schooling can help students and teachers who find it hard to wait for summer vacation.

Staying Busy in the
SUMMER

Some students might get bored during a long summer vacation, but others use the time to stay busy with family trips, summer camps, and summer jobs. Year-round schooling makes it hard to do these things because students are in school for most of the summer. This can also hurt businesses such as camps and **amusement parks** that are busiest during summer vacations.

Year-round schooling is also hard for families with children in different schools. Older children might not be around to babysit their younger brothers and sisters if they go to different kinds of schools or are on different tracks.

Know the Facts!

During the summer of 2016, 35 percent of American teenagers had jobs or were looking for jobs.

Many young people use their summer vacations to play sports or do another activity that can require traveling. Year-round schooling makes it harder to do these activities.

Helping with
OVERCROWDING

One of the most popular reasons for switching to year-round schooling is overcrowding in schools. Many U.S. schools, especially in cities, are too crowded. Multi-track, year-round schooling helps spread out the number of students in school at one time. Only some students are in the school building at any given time during the year.

Keeping schools open for learning all year round also keeps the buildings in use. Schools are often left unused in the summer months, which is seen by many as a waste of space.

Know the Facts!

As of 2012, more than half of all year-round schools were elementary schools.

When students go to school all year round, it makes the best use of the school building.

COSTS

Keeping schools open all year round isn't always easy. It's more expensive to keep them open if they're generally closed all summer. It costs money to keep the lights on and the air conditioning running during times when the building used to be closed.

In addition, some school buildings aren't meant to be used all year. Schools in some parts of the United States don't have air conditioning. This is fine when students aren't in the building for the hottest months of the year. However, the buildings would be too hot if students were there during the summer.

Know the Facts!

Summer is often seen as the time to **repair** parts of school buildings that need fixing. Without a summer vacation, it's harder to find time to do these repairs.

It would cost some schools a lot of money to get the air conditioning systems they need to be open all year.

Looking at
BOTH SIDES

Many other countries use a year-round schooling system, but only around 4 percent of U.S. public schools are year-round schools. Year-round schooling is debated by people across the United States, and people have many different points of view about it.

People on both sides of the debate believe they're arguing for what's best for students, teachers, and families. However, there's still no real **proof** that one way of schooling is better than the other. After learning the facts about year-round schooling, do you think it's a good idea?

Know the Facts!

Most year-round schools in the United States have more than 200 students.

Should students go to school all year round?

YES

- Students have less time to forget what they learned.

- Teachers don't have to spend as much time reviewing and can spend time on new lessons.

- Having more breaks helps with student and teacher burnout.

- Students can get bored during a long summer vacation.

- Multi-track systems can help make schools less crowded and keep the buildings in use all year.

NO

- Students still forget over short breaks, which means teachers need to review more often.

- There's no solid proof that year-round schooling leads to better grades.

- It can be hard for parents when their children have different breaks from school.

- Students can't take long family vacations, go to summer camp, or get a summer job.

- It can cost more for schools to stay open during the summer.

Making a chart such as this one can help you form your own opinions about the world around you.

GLOSSARY

amusement park: A place with rides and games that people go to for fun.

debate: An argument or discussion about an issue, generally between two sides. Also, to take part in such an argument or discussion.

proof: Something that shows that something else is true or correct.

repair: To fix. Also, the act or result of fixing.

review: To study or look at something again.

stressful: Causing strong feelings of worry.

traditional: Following what's been done for a long time.

For More
INFORMATION

WEBSITES

'Always Ready to Go Back': Could Students Benefit from Year-Round School?
www.pbs.org/newshour/show/always-ready-go-back-students-may-benefit-year-round-schooling
This PBS video follows a family whose children go to a year-round school.

"What to Do if You Don't Like School"
kidshealth.org/en/kids/hate-school.html
This KidsHealth article offers advice for students who don't like school and are dealing with school-related stress.

BOOKS

Lee, Sally. *School Long Ago and Today.* North Mankato, MN: Capstone Press, 2015.

Robertson, J. Jean. *Everyone Goes to School.* Vero Beach, FL: Rourke Educational Media, 2016.

Smith, Penny, and Zahavit Shalev. *A School Like Mine: A Celebration of Schools Around the World.* New York, NY: DK Publishing, 2016.

Publisher's note to educators and parents: Our editors have carefully reviewed these websites to ensure that they are suitable for students. Many websites change frequently, however, and we cannot guarantee that a site's future contents will continue to meet our high standards of quality and educational value. Be advised that students should be closely supervised whenever they access the Internet.

INDEX

A
amusement parks, 14

B
babysit, 14
bored, 12, 14, 21
burnout, 12, 21

C
costs, 18, 19, 21

E
Education Week, 8

F
forgotten facts, 9

H
higher grades, 10

L
Los Angeles,
    California, 10

M
multi-track, 6, 16, 21

O
overcrowding, 16

R
repair, 18
reviewing, 8, 9, 10,
    21

S
short breaks, 4, 12,
    21
single track, 6
summer camp, 14,
    21
summer job, 14, 21
summer vacations, 4,
    5, 8, 12, 13, 14,
    15, 18, 21

T
teachers, 4, 6, 8, 9,
    10, 12, 13, 20,
    21
traditional schools, 6